HOLT SCIENCE
SKILLBOOK

Joseph Abruscato   Joan Wade Fossaceca   Jack Hassard   Donald Peck

Holt, Rinehart and Winston, Publishers   New York · Toronto · Mexico City · London · Sydney · Tokyo

D1319351

THE AUTHORS

Joseph Abruscato
Associate Dean
College of Education and Social Services
University of Vermont
Burlington, Vermont

Jack Hassard
Professor
College of Education
Georgia State University
Atlanta, Georgia

Joan Wade Fossaceca
Teacher
Pointview Elementary School
Westerville City Schools
Westerville, Ohio

Donald Peck
Supervisor of Science
Woodbridge Township School District
Woodbridge, New Jersey

Art Credits

Gary Allen, pages 2, 7, 8, 19, 46, 50, 52, 55
Morissa Lipstein, pages 13, 38, 41, 49, 54, 67
Joel Snyder, pages 1, 4, 6, 12, 13, 14, 26, 27, 29, 30, 31, 32, 34, 44, 63, 75, 78, 86, 88
Vantage Art, Inc., pages 5, 11, 28, 42, 63, 66, 68

Photo Credits

HRW photos by **Russell Dian** appear on page 35.
Unit 2: p. 15—Courtesy of the American Museum of Natural History;
p. 21 top left—Jeff Albertson/Stock, Boston, top right—Grant Heilman, bottom—
Lynn McLaren/Rapho/Photo Researchers, Inc.; p. 22 left—Gerhard E. Gscheidle/
Peter Arnold, Inc., right—Grant Heilman; p. 25—Werner H. Müller/Peter
Arnold, Inc.; p. 28—Rue/Monkmeyer Press
Unit 4: p. 45—NASA; p. 47—NASA; p. 51—NASA; p. 53 left—Dennis Milon,
right—NASA; p. 56—NASA; p. 57—NASA; p. 58—NASA
Unit 5: p. 71 left—Tom McHugh/Photo Researchers, Inc.; p. 71 right—Southern
California Edison Company; p. 72 top left—Apple Computer, Inc., top right—
Biophoto Associates/Photo Researchers, Inc.; p. 72 bottom left—Cary Wolinsky/Stock,
Boston; bottom right—Apple Computer, Inc.

Cover Photo

David Muench/The Image Bank

Copyright © 1986, 1984 by Holt, Rinehart and Winston, Publishers
All Rights Reserved
Printed in the United States of America
ISBN 0-03-003448-5
6789   019   7654

Table of Contents

Chapter 1 What Is a Living Thing?

Chapter 2 How Living Things Grow

Chapter 3 Simple Living Things

Chapter 4 Rocks

Chapter 5 Changing Rocks

Chapter 6 Fossils

Chapter 7 Matter

Chapter 8 Heat

Chapter 9 Matter in Water and Air

Chapter 10 The Earth and the Moon

Chapter 11 The Sun and the Stars

Chapter 12 Journey to the Planets

Chapter 13 Magnets

Chapter 14 Electricity

Chapter 15 Using Electricity

Chapter 16 The Forest and the Grassland

Chapter 17 The Desert and the Tundra

Chapter 18 Water Habitats

Name _____ Date _____

CHAPTER 1

WHAT IS A LIVING THING?

Section 1-1. LIVING AND NON-LIVING THINGS

Each picture shows an object that is not alive. On the lines below the pictures, tell how the objects shown are like living things. Then tell how they are different from living things.

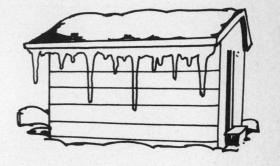

_____

_____

_____

_____

_____

_____

_____

_____

Name _____ Date _____

Section 1-2. WHAT ARE LIVING THINGS MADE OF?

A. Color the diagram of a plant cell.
1. Color the cell wall green.
2. Color the cell membrane red.
3. Color the nucleus brown.
4. Color the liquid in the cell blue.

B. Write the name of each part of the cell on the line that points to the part.

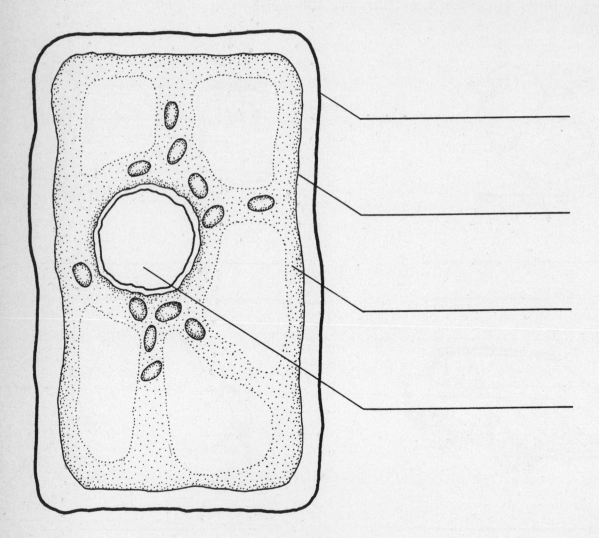

CHAPTER 1

SKILLS EXERCISE

BUILDING SCIENCE VOCABULARY

Fill in the blanks with the correct words from the list.

Living things are not like _____
things. Living things need _____ in
order to grow. Animals can _____ from
place to place. Plants cannot, but they can turn their
_____ or branches to get sunlight. All
living things can _____ to make other
living things like themselves.

All living things are made of _____.
It takes millions of cells to make one plant or
one animal. Plant cells are different from animal cells.
Plant cells have a cell _____. Animal
cells do not. Both animal cells and plant cells
are surrounded by a cell _____. This
holds the cell together. The control center for a
cell is its _____. It directs the growth
and _____ of the cell. The nucleus floats
in a jelly-like liquid called _____.

non-living

cells

wall

leaves

nucleus

food

reproduce

move

cytoplasm

reproduction

membrane

CHAPTER 1

ACTIVITY

WHAT DOES A PLANT CELL LOOK LIKE?

A. You will need a lettuce leaf, an onion ring, iodine, a microscope, a microscope slide, and a cover slip.

B. Peel the thin skin off the inside of a lettuce leaf. Put it on a microscope slide.

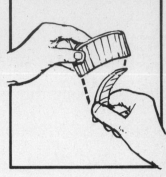

C. Place a drop of iodine on the skin and cover it with a cover slip.

D. Look at the lettuce skin through a microscope.
   1. What shape are the lettuce skin cells?

   _____

   _____

   2. The nucleus will be either brown or yellow.

   What is it shaped like? _____

   _____

E. Make a slide with the skin from the inside of an onion ring, the same way you made the lettuce slide. Look at the slide through the microscope.
   3. How are the onion skin cells and the lettuce

   cells alike? _____

   _____

F. Look for some very tiny cells that are something like a doughnut. These cells have holes in the middle that open and close. The plant breathes through these cells.
   4. How many "breathing" cells did you find?

   _____

CHAPTER 2

HOW LIVING THINGS GROW

Section 2-1. WHERE DO CELLS COME FROM?

Everything starts from just one cell. Did you ever wonder how whales, mosquitoes, mushrooms, and redwoods can all have so many? Imagine that you have a funny kind of cell called a "clock cell." Every hour each cell divides in two. Starting with one cell, there will be two cells in one hour, four cells in two hours, and so on.

How many cells do you think there will be in 12 hours? To find out, double the number of cells for each hour around the 12-hour clock.

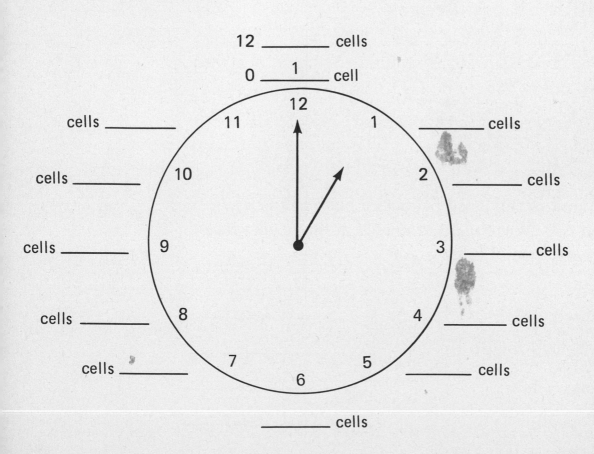

12 _____ cells

0 ___1___ cell

cells _____

cells _____

cells _____

cells _____

cells _____

_____ cells

_____ cells

_____ cells

_____ cells

_____ cells

_____ cells

Section 2-2. SINGLE CELLS AND HOW THEY DIVIDE
Section 2-3. SPECIAL CELLS

A. The pictures below show different times in the life cycle of a plant. Start with the picture of the flower with the bee on top. Draw lines that connect the pictures in the order that the plant grows. When you finish, you will have drawn 5 lines.

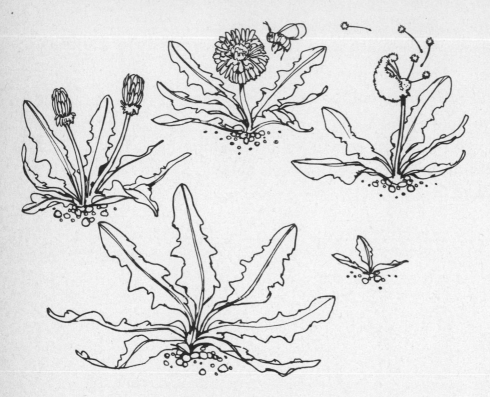

B. Each kind of cell listed below is a plant cell or an animal cell. Write *plant* or *animal* in the blank space after each type of cell.

1. Muscle cells _____

2. Cells with root hairs _____

3. Bone cells _____

4. Skin cells _____

5. Cells with chloroplasts _____

CHAPTER 2

SKILLS EXERCISE

WRITING SKILLS

Complete the story below on your own:

Ladies and gentlemen, this is an exciting trip! Our microscopic inner-space ship, the *Micron*, is speeding down the inside of Gulliver's arm! Everywhere we see cells: blood cells, muscle cells, bone cells . . .

platelets

red blood cells

white blood cells

_____

_____

_____

_____

_____

_____

_____

_____

_____

_____

_____

_____

_____

CHAPTER 2

ACTIVITY

WHERE DO YOU FIND ONE-CELLED ANIMALS?

Pond water contains tiny animal-like creatures that have only one cell. You can grow some of these creatures and look at them under a microscope.

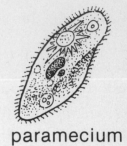

paramecium

A. You will need a glass jar, a microscope, a microscope slide, a cover slip, a soda straw, dry grass, and water from a pond or brook.

B. Fill your jar about half full of the pond or brook water. Put a handful of dry grass in the water.

C. Set the jar in a warm, dimly lit place for about 10 days.

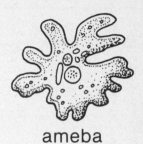

ameba

D. Lower one end of the soda straw close to the bottom of the jar. Place your finger over the top of the straw to hold the water in. Use the straw to move a drop of water from the bottom of the jar to the slide.

E. Put the cover slip over the water drop and place the slide on the microscope. Look through the microscope. Move the slide until you see small creatures darting around.

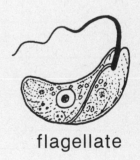

flagellate

1. What do the creatures look like?

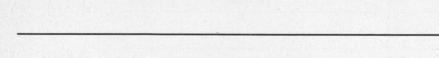

_____

2. In what area do you find most of the creatures?

_____

3. Why do you think they stay there?

_____

CHAPTER 3

SIMPLE LIVING THINGS

Section 3-1. ONE-CELLED ORGANISMS

Do you know what these one-celled organisms are? Write
their names.

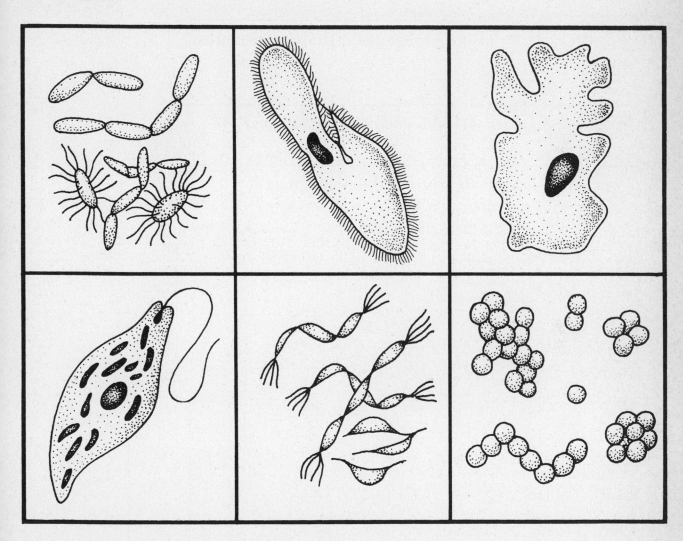

Which of the above are protozoans? Write
one sentence about each protozoan.

Section 3-2. OTHER ONE-CELLED ORGANISMS

A number of one-celled organisms living in the same place are called a population. They are a lot like people. All populations change just like ours does. The graph shows the population growth of a simple organism compared with time. Study the graph and answer the questions.

1. How many organisms were there on the first day?

    _____

2. On which days did the number of organisms grow the most?

    _____

3. What happened to the population after 20 days?

    _____

4. How many organisms were in the population at

    a. 10 days? _____

    b. 15 days? _____

    c. 20 days? _____

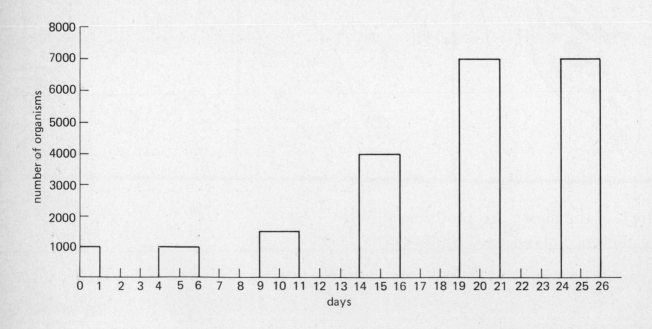

Section 3-3. SIMPLE FOOD USERS

The words in the sentences below are out of order. Put
the words in the right order so that they make sense. You
will learn something about molds and other simple
organisms.

1. that organism a simple food is spoils mold.

    _____

2. cloth grows on mold that is kind of a mildew.

    _____

3. a organism is bread to yeast used make simple.

    _____

4. soil turns mold and leaves into dead wood.

    _____

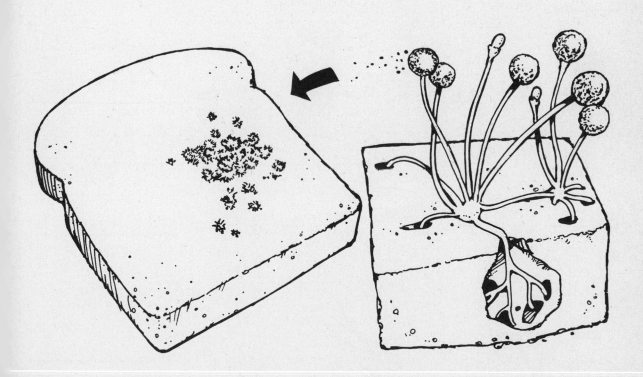

CHAPTER 3

SKILLS EXERCISE

BUILDING SCIENCE VOCABULARY

Below are four puzzles. The answer to each is a kind of simple organism. Can you solve the puzzles?

Example 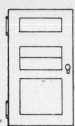 — **or** + **ugh** + = ___doughnut___

1. 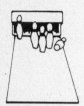 — **e** + **G** = _____

2. — **LL** +  = _____

3. —  +  — **i** = _____

4.  +  = _____

Name _____ Date _____

COMPARING AND CONTRASTING, READING ILLUSTRATIONS

This cartoon shows a factory that is something like a green
plant cell. Look at it carefully. Then answer the questions.

1. What part of a plant cell is like **A** in the cartoon?

   _____

2. **B** is the factory's office. How is it like the

   nucleus of a cell? _____

   _____

   _____

3. This factory and a plant cell make the same

   product. What is it? _____

4. What three things do both the factory and the plant

   cell need to make their product? _____

   _____

5. Cell walls have gates in them just like the factory

   wall. What is happening at the wall in **D**? _____

   _____

CHAPTER 3

ACTIVITY

WHERE DOES MOLD GROW?

A. You will need a large glass jar with a lid, soil, an orange peel, a banana peel, cheese, and bread.

B. Lay the jar on its side. Put some clay under it so it will not roll. Spread some soil in the jar. (Note: Use soil from outdoors, not sterilized potting soil.)

C. Place a small piece of bread on the soil. Then add a piece of cheese, a piece of orange peel, and a piece of banana peel.

D. Put the jar in a dim, warm place. Look at it each day for two weeks.

1. On what food did the mold grow first?

    _____

2. Do different kinds of mold grow on different

    foods? _____

3. How are the molds different?

    _____

CHAPTER 4

ROCKS

Section 4-1. **OBSERVING ROCKS**

A. List at least three properties for each rock shown

here. _____

_____

_____

B. What is a mineral? Give an example of a mineral.

_____

_____

_____

C. On a separate sheet of paper write a short letter to a
friend. Describe the rocks you saw on a hike in the
mountains. Use the following words: *property,
mineral, rock, quartz, halite.*

Name _____ Date _____

Section 4-2. USING ROCKS

A. Suppose your teacher gives you a rock in a paper bag. What properties of the rock could you discover? You cannot open the bag. But you can touch it.

_____

_____

B. What kind of rock would make a good arrowhead?

Why? _____

_____

C. Rock **A** scratches rock **B**. Which rock is harder? _____

D. Renumber the following list of rocks from softest to hardest. Write your numbers in the blanks at the right.

1. scratches a penny but not a knife   _____

2. scratches glass   _____

3. will not scratch your fingernail   _____

E. Draw a picture showing one way people use rocks.

CHAPTER 4
SKILLS EXERCISE

WRITING SKILLS

A cinquain is a poem that has five lines. A Japanese cinquain is written in the following way:

line 1	one word	Sand
line 2	a property of line 1	shiny and bright
line 3	a feeling you have about line 1	nice to play in
line 4	another property of line 1	tan and black
line 5	a meaning of line 1	tiny pebbles

This sample cinquain is:

> sand
> shiny and bright
> nice to play in
> tan and black
> tiny pebbles

Below are the first lines for two cinquains. Complete each cinquain.

Rock _____   Mineral _____

_____   _____

_____   _____

_____   _____

_____   _____

CHAPTER 4

ACTIVITY

COLLECTING ROCKS

In this Activity, you will collect different rocks and observe their properties.

A. You will need a piece of cardboard, a marking pen, and glue.

B. Collect as many different kinds of rocks as you can find. Look around your home or school.

C. Glue each rock to the cardboard. Write a number for each rock on the cardboard next to the rock.

D. Look at each rock. In the chart below, record how it looks and feels.

Rock	Property			
	Size	Shape	Feel	Color
1				
2				
3				
4				
5				

Name _____ Date _____

CHAPTER 5
CHANGING ROCKS

Section 5-1. WEATHERING

A. How can rocks be weathered? Describe the way shown
in each of the pictures.

       1   2   3

1. _____

2. _____

3. _____

B. How can the following change rocks?

   1. freezing _____

      _____

      _____

   2. carbon dioxide _____

      _____

   3. roots _____

      _____

19

Section 5-2. SOIL

A. Read each sentence below. Decide if it is true or false. If the sentence is true, write the word true on the line next to it. If the sentence is false, write the word or words that makes it true and underline the incorrect word or words.

_____ 1. Soil is made from pieces of broken rock.

_____ 2. There is only one kind of soil.

_____ 3. Soil can contain dead plants and animals.

_____ 4. Humus is made of parts of dead plants and animals.

_____ 5. Subsoil is mostly large pieces of rock.

_____ 6. Sandy soil contains humus.

_____ 7 Sandy soil does not hold water very well.

_____ 8. Clay soil is made of very small pieces of different minerals.

B. Why is soil important to plants, animals, and people?

_____

_____

_____

_____

_____

Name _____ Date _____

Section 5-3. EROSION

A. Name the type of erosion taking place in each of these
pictures.

1. _____

2. _____

3. _____

B. What is conservation? _____

_____

C. What is one way to slow down erosion? Describe how
this method works.

_____

_____

_____

_____

21

Name _____ Date _____

CHAPTER 5

SKILLS EXERCISE

WRITING SKILLS

Look at the pictures below. On the lines above them, write a letter to a local newspaper or civic group telling how you feel about the events taking place.

Date _____

Dear _____,

_____

_____

_____

_____

Sincerely,

_____

BUILDING SCIENCE VOCABULARY

Use the clues listed below to complete the crossword puzzle.

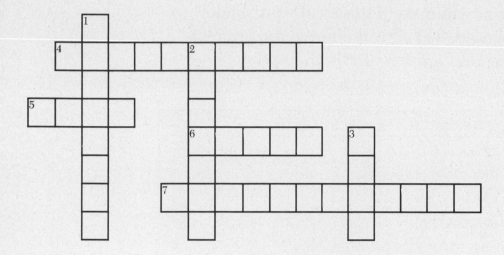

Down
1. Broken rock carried away by wind and water.
2. Carrying away or wearing down of rocks and soil.
3. The type of soil that holds water very well.

Across
4. Breaking rocks into smaller pieces by rain, ice, and plants.
5. Tiny pieces of rocks and minerals.
6. The type of soil that does not hold water well.
7. Ways of taking care of the land.

CHAPTER 5
ACTIVITY

MAKING AN EROSION SURVEY

In this Activity, you will make a survey of your school grounds or neighborhood. You will observe the area for signs of weathering and erosion. To do the survey, refer to this chart.

Weathering and Erosion Chart
Weathering
1. Tiny plants growing on rocks.
2. Cracks in rocks.
3. Cracked sidewalks.
4. Water dripping on rocks or sidewalks.
Erosion
1. Water flowing in a stream.
2. Soil blowing in the wind.
3. Soil not covered with plants.
4. Piles of sand.

On a separate sheet of paper, make a small map of the area you are going to survey. As you find evidence for weathering or erosion, mark the location on your map. In the space below, list the examples of weathering and erosion.

Weathering

_____

_____

_____

Erosion

_____

_____

_____

Name _____ Date _____

CHAPTER 6

FOSSILS

Section 6-1. FOSSIL HUNTING

A. This is a fossil shell. It once lived in the ocean. How
    do you think this shell became a fossil? List the steps
    below.

1. _____

2. _____

3. _____

4. _____

5. _____

B. What can scientists learn from fossils? _____

    _____

C. How can a fossil be made from the following?

    1. Amber _____

       _____

    2. Tar pit _____

       _____

    3. Ice _____

       _____

Section 6-2. FOSSIL STORIES

A. Each picture shows life as it may have been long ago.
   Describe each picture.

1.

2.

3.

4.

1. _____

2. _____

   _____

3. _____

4. _____

B. Which picture shows what the earliest form of life was
   like? Explain.

   _____

   _____

   _____

   _____

Name _____ Date _____

Section 6-3. DINOSAURS

In this exercise, you are going to be a detective. Some fossil footprints have been found. They are shown in the drawing. Your job is to figure out what happened. Use the questions to help you.

1. How many dinosaurs made the footprints? _____

2. Which way were they moving? _____

   _____

   _____

3. Was either of the dinosaurs running? How do you

   know? _____

   _____

   _____

4. Was the soil moist or dry on the day the prints were

   made? _____

   _____

5. What might have happened where the prints meet?

   _____

   _____

   _____

   _____

6. Why is there only one set of prints leaving the area?

   _____

   _____

   _____

   _____

CHAPTER 6

SKILLS EXERCISE

OBSERVING, MEASURING, INFERRING

This picture shows a population of fossils. Each fossil shell is the same kind of animal. In this exercise, you will use your observing skills to find out about these fossils.

On a separate sheet of paper, answer these questions about this picture.

1. How many fossils are in this population?
2. Describe the shape of the fossil shells.
3. Measure the lengths of 10 of the fossils.
4. What are the sizes of the biggest and the smallest shells?
5. Which shell do you think is the average size? How big is this shell?
6. How do you think this animal lived?

cm 1 2 3 4 5 6 7 8 9 10

WRITING SKILLS

Suppose you found yourself in the scene shown below. It's a long time ago. This is the time of the dinosaurs. Pretend you are a science reporter for the city newspaper. Your task is to describe as best you can what it is like to be with the dinosaurs. Write your story in a newspaper column. Be sure to give your story a title, for example, "A Day with the Dinosaurs."

Title: _____

_____

_____

_____

_____

_____

_____

_____

_____

_____

_____

CHAPTER 6

ACTIVITY

FIGURING OUT THE PAST

Make a small drawing of each of the following dinosaurs, and tell at least two facts about it.

Brontosaurus   **Tyrannosaurus**

_____   _____
_____   _____
_____   _____

Allosaurus   **Stegosaurus**

_____   _____
_____   _____
_____   _____

CHAPTER 7

MATTER

Section 7-1. SOLIDS, LIQUIDS, AND GASES

Each of these pictures shows matter that is a solid, a liquid, or a gas. Write the form of matter under each picture.

Name _____ Date _____

Section 7-2. HEATING MATTER

A. In the box at the right, draw how the glass would look
   if the liquid in it evaporated.

B. In the box at the right, draw how the balloon would
   look if the air in it were heated.

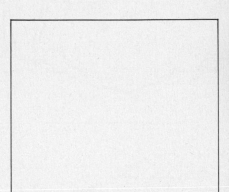

C. In the box at the right, draw what will happen if the
   ice cube is not placed in the freezer.

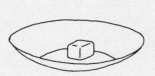

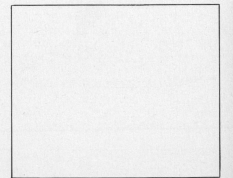

Section 7-3. COOLING MATTER

One thing can cause something else to happen. The thing
that happens is called an effect. Read the lists of causes
and effects. Then write the missing causes or effects in the
blank spaces.

CAUSE	EFFECT
1. _____ _____ _____ _____ _____	Water condenses on the outside of a glass of ice water.
2. The freezer cools a tray of water to 0° Celsius.	_____ _____ _____ _____
3. Hot liquid iron is poured into a container and left to cool.	_____ _____ _____ _____
4. _____ _____ _____ _____	Steam condenses into liquid water.

Name _____ Date _____

Section 7-4. MATTER CHANGES SIZE

A. Fill in the blanks with the correct words from the list.

heated   cooled

expands   contract

When water is cooled, it _____. But

most gases, solids, and liquids _____

when they are cooled. If you _____ a

balloon, it would expand. A sidewalk would contract

if it were _____.

B. This series of pictures shows a balloon that is being heated. Number the pictures from warmest to coolest (1, 2, 3).

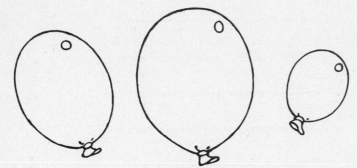

C. In these pictures one jar lid is being cooled. The other jar lid is being heated. Write "easier" under the picture that shows the lid that would be easier to take off.

34

CHAPTER 7

SKILLS EXERCISE

READING ILLUSTRATIONS

On the lines next to each drawing, write a sentence about what is happening in the drawing and why.

1.

1. _____
   _____
   _____
   _____
   _____
   _____

2.

2. _____
   _____
   _____
   _____
   _____
   _____

3.

3. _____
   _____
   _____
   _____
   _____
   _____

CHAPTER 7

ACTIVITY

OBSERVING EVAPORATION

Evaporation is the changing of matter from a liquid into a gas. Try this evaporation Activity.

A. You will need two glass bowls and water.

B. Place the same amount of water in each bowl.

C. Place one bowl in a cool place and the other one in a warm place.

D. Look at the amount of water in the bowls each day for 3 or 4 days.

   1. Which bowl had less water in it at the end of

      the Activity? _____

      _____

      _____

      _____

   2. Where did the water go? _____

      _____

      _____

   3. What name is given to water that is a gas in

      the air? _____

   4. Why did the bowl in the warm place have less

      water in it? _____

      _____

      _____

      _____

CHAPTER 8

HEAT

Section 8-1. SOURCES OF HEAT

In Chapter 8, you learned that some people use the heat
from the sun to heat their homes. The homes are built in
a special way, or new parts are added to them. In the box
below draw how your home would look if heat from the
sun were used to heat it.

Section 8-2. MEASURING HEAT

These pictures show activities that take place at different temperatures. Look at the pictures and the thermometers to the right of the pictures. Then write the temperature shown on each thermometer on the blank line under each picture.

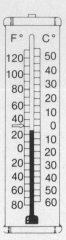

_____

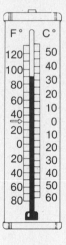

_____

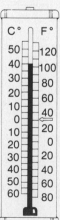

_____

CHAPTER 8

SKILLS EXERCISE

BUILDING SCIENCE VOCABULARY

Use the clues listed below to complete the crossword puzzle.

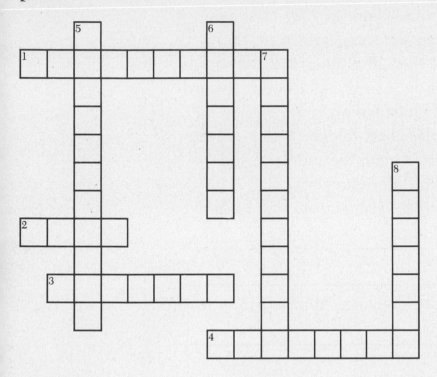

ACROSS

1. A type of thermometer scale.
2. Anything that can be burned to produce heat.
3. Units used to measure temperature.
4. 0° C or 32° F.

DOWN

5. Used to measure how hot or cold something is.
6. A type of thermometer scale.
7. How hot or cold something is.
8. 100° C or 212° F.

CHAPTER 8

ACTIVITY

RECORDING CHANGES IN TEMPERATURE

A. You will need a thermometer, crayons, a pencil, and a sheet of paper.

B. Place the thermometer somewhere in your classroom.

C. Each day, for 5 days, read the temperature on the thermometer. Do this at the same times each day, once in the morning and once in the afternoon. Record the temperatures on the chart below.

D. Use the information on the chart to draw a line graph like the one shown below. Graph the morning and afternoon temperatures in different colors.

  1. How did the temperature change from day to day?

    _____

    _____

  2. How did the temperature change from morning to afternoon? _____

    _____

  3. Why do you think the changes occurred?

    _____

    _____

day	morning temperature	afternoon temperature
1		
2		
3		
4		
5		

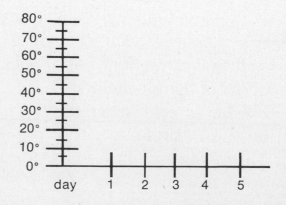

CHAPTER 9

MATTER IN WATER AND AIR

Section 9-1. WATER CHANGES MATTER
Pretend that you are going to make a pitcher of lemonade.
Below is a list of steps you have to do, but the list is out
of order. Number the steps in the order that you would
do them.

_____ Add sugar.

_____ Squeeze the juice from lemons.

_____ Add ice cubes.

_____ Stir.

_____ Get a pitcher and several lemons.

_____ Add lemon juice to the pitcher.

_____ Fill the pitcher 3/4 full of water.

_____ Drink and enjoy it!

Section 9-2. AIR CHANGES MATTER

Sally covered a burning candle with different-sized jars.
The graph tells how long her candle burned under each
jar. Look at the graph. Then answer the questions below.

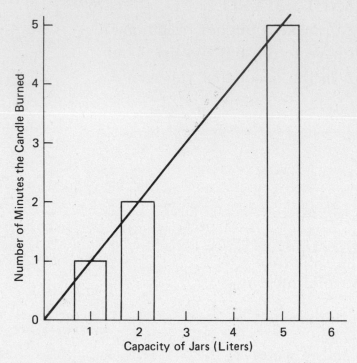

1. How long did the candle burn under the 1-liter jar?

   _____

2. How long did the candle burn under the 2-liter jar?

   _____

3. How long did the candle burn under the 5-liter jar?

   _____

4. Sally could not find a 4-liter jar. How long does the
   graph tell you that a candle would burn under a

   4-liter jar? _____

5. How much air did the candle need to keep burning for

   5 minutes? _____

6. How much air would the candle need to keep burning

   for 3 minutes? _____

42

CHAPTER 9

SKILLS EXERCISE

BUILDING SCIENCE VOCABULARY

Fill in the blanks with the correct words from the list. You
may use a word more than once.

burns	gases	warm
heat	light	oxygen
dissolve	matter	solid
stirring	solution	iron

Water changes some kinds of matter. Many kinds of

matter _____ in water. They dissolve

easier when the water is _____.

_____ also helps to make things dissolve.

When a _____ or liquid is dissolved in a

liquid, they make a _____.

   Air changes some kinds of _____, too.

One of the _____ in air is oxygen. When

some kinds of matter become hot, the _____

causes them to burn. When something _____,

it gives off heat and _____. When oxygen

changes metals like copper and _____,

it makes _____. But it does not make

any _____.

CHAPTER 9

ACTIVITY

MAKING RUST

A. You will need steel wool, aluminum foil, water, vinegar water, and ammonia water.

B. Make 4 bowls out of the aluminum foil. Each bowl should be about the size of your hand.

C. Roll steel wool into 4 balls. Each ball should be about 3 cm across.

D. Wet 1 ball with water and put it in a bowl. Wet the second ball with ammonia water and put it in a bowl. Wet the third ball with vinegar water and put it in a bowl. Leave the fourth ball dry and put it in a bowl.

E. Look at each ball the next day. Try to break each ball apart.

  1. Did the dry ball rust? _____

  2. Did the ball in plain water rust? _____

  3. Did the ball in ammonia water rust? _____

  _____

  4. Did the ball in vinegar water rust? _____

  5. Which ball rusted the most? _____

  _____

| steel wool and water | steel wool, water, and ammonia | steel wool, water, and vinegar | steel wool |

CHAPTER 10

THE EARTH AND THE MOON

Section 10-1. THE BLUE PLANET

A. Label the four parts of the earth that are shown in the picture.

B. Which planet in the solar system is called the blue

planet? Explain your answer. _____

_____

_____

C. Draw a diagram using the earth and sun to explain revolution.

Name _____ Date _____

Section 10-2. MOON WATCH

A. Why do we say the moon is a satellite of the earth?

_____

_____

B. Make a diagram that shows the moon revolving around
the earth. How long does it take for 1 revolution of

the moon? _____

C. Where does the moon's light come from? _____

D. Look at the drawing below. Why does the moon

change shape as it goes around the earth? _____

_____

_____

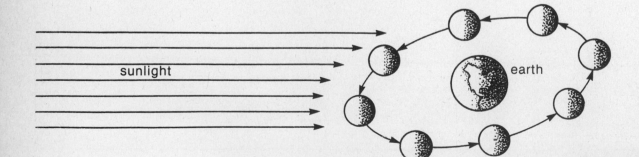

Name _____ Date _____

Section 10-3. EXPLORING THE MOON

A. How is the moon different from the earth? List at

least three ways. _____

_____

_____

B. In this picture, what are the small bowl-shaped

features? _____

C. In the box below make a drawing to show what causes
craters on the moon.

CHAPTER 10

SKILLS EXERCISE

BUILDING SCIENCE VOCABULARY

Use the clues listed below to complete the crossword puzzle.

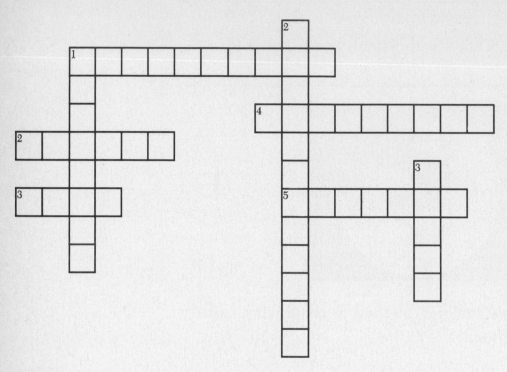

ACROSS

1. The movement of one object around another object.
2. A solid body in space that does not give off its own light.
3. An imaginary line running through the earth from the North Pole to the South Pole.
4. A small planet that revolves around another planet.
5. Bowl-shaped holes made by objects traveling in space that hit the moon or the earth.

DOWN

1. The spinning of the earth on its axis.
2. Ice and snow that cover land near the top and bottom of the earth (3 words).
3. A path around an object in space.

Name _____ Date _____

CHAPTER 10

ACTIVITY

DOES THE MOON CHANGE SIZE?
When the moon rises, it plays a trick on your eyes. In this
Activity, you will find out what this trick is.

A. You will need a ruler and a newspaper or an almanac.

B. Use the newspaper or almanac to find out when the
moon will rise. Then go outside and watch the moon as
it rises.

C. Hold the ruler in front of you and measure the width
of the moon.

    1. What is the width of the moon? _____

    _____

D. Later the same night repeat step **C**.

    2. What seemed to happen to the moon? _____

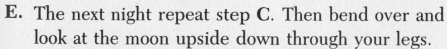

    _____

    3. What did you find out when you measured it a

    second time? _____

E. The next night repeat step **C**. Then bend over and
look at the moon upside down through your legs.

    4. What seemed to happen to the moon when you

    looked at it upside down? _____

    5. What trick does the moon play on your eyes?

_____

CHAPTER 10

ACTIVITY

MOON STUDY

In this Activity, you are going to observe the moon on a clear night.

A. You will need 2 large index cards, a flashlight, and a pencil.

B. On an index card, draw the landscape around your home. Show the landscape from the southeast (SE) to the southwest (SW).

C. When it begins to get dark, find the moon. Draw it on your card.

D. Repeat step **C** every hour for at least two hours.

   1. In what direction is the moon moving? _____

   _____

   2. Did it change shape? _____

E. Make a second drawing of the landscape on the other card. Repeat your observations of the moon the next night.

   3. Was the moon in the same place at the same time

   the next evening? _____

   _____

Name _____ Date _____

CHAPTER 11

THE SUN AND THE STARS

Section 11-1. THE SUN

A. Look at these pictures of the sun and the earth. Under
the pictures write at least three ways that the sun and
the earth are different.

 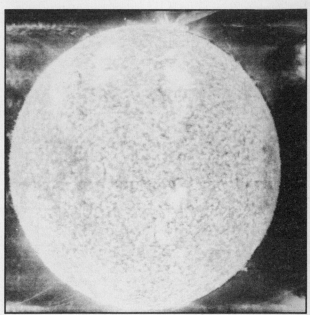

_____

_____

_____

_____

B. What are the dark spots on the surface of the sun?

_____

C. How are these dark spots different from other places

on the sun? _____

D. What keeps the earth in its orbit around the sun?

_____

Name _____ Date _____

Section 11-2. THE NIGHT SKY

A. Look at the constellations shown below. Name each
   constellation and write a sentence about each one.

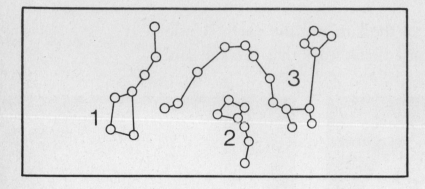

1. _____

   _____

   _____

2. _____

   _____

3. _____

B. A student told a friend, "I saw an object in the sky last
   night. It traveled very fast. It looked like a flash of
   light!" What do you think the student saw? Explain
   your answer.

   _____

   _____

   _____

   _____

C. Which constellations should you use to find the North

   Star? _____

CHAPTER 11

SKILLS EXERCISE

BUILDING SCIENCE VOCABULARY, WRITING SKILLS
Look at the pictures below. Then write a short paragraph about each.

◀ A

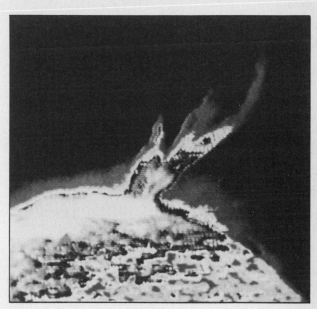

B ▲

A. _____

_____

_____

_____

_____

B. _____

_____

_____

CHAPTER 11

ACTIVITY

DRAWING A SKY MAP

What objects in the night sky are above your home? Find out and draw a sky map.

A. You will need black construction paper, white crayons (or chalk), and a flashlight.

B. Go outside at night with a friend or an adult.

C. Find the moon and some of the constellations you have read about in your text.

D. Draw what you see on the black paper. Your friend should hold the flashlight over the paper so you can see well.

E. Mark the location of the moon as well as the stars on your map.

F. Bring your sky map to class. Compare your map with your classmates' maps.

Name _____ Date _____

CHAPTER 12

JOURNEY TO THE PLANETS

Section 12-1. THE SOLAR SYSTEM

A. Which of these diagrams correctly shows the positions
of some of the planets in our solar system?

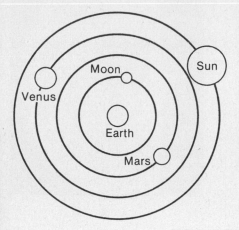
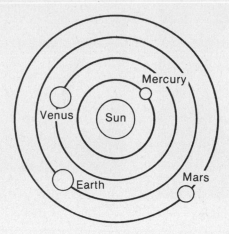

_____

B. Why do you think our system of planets is called the

"solar system"? _____

_____

_____

C. Make a list of the planets found in these two groups:

Group A. The inner planets: _____

_____

Group B. The outer planets: _____

_____

D. What is one difference between the inner and outer

planets? _____

_____

Name _____ Date _____

Section 12-2. THE EARTH-LIKE PLANETS

Pretend you are a scientist observing pictures of some of
the planets. Look at these pictures. What planets are
shown? Describe each planet.

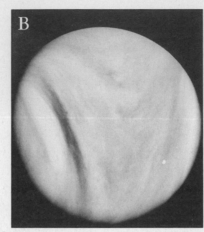
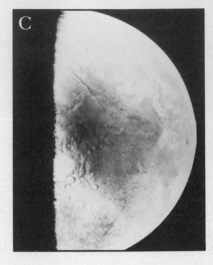

A. _____

_____

_____

_____

_____

B. _____

_____

_____

_____

C. _____

_____

_____

_____

_____

Name _____ Date _____

Section 12-3. THE GIANT PLANETS

A. The photographs show pictures of two of the largest
planets in our solar system. Name each planet.

1. _____   2. _____

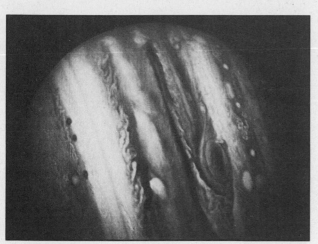   

B. Which of the giant planets is described below?

   1. The planet with the Great Red Spot _____
   2. It takes 30 years for this planet to revolve around

      the sun. _____

   3. This planet is tilted on its side. _____
   4. It takes 165 years for this planet to travel

      around the sun. _____

C. Describe each of these satellites of Jupiter.

   1. Callisto _____

      _____

   2. Ganymede _____

   3. Europa _____

      _____

   4. Io _____

57

Name _____ Date _____

CHAPTER 12

SKILLS EXERCISE

READING ILLUSTRATIONS

Look at each picture. Then choose the best title for it from the list below. Write the title under each picture.

Astronaut Rides Rover on Moon
The Largest Planet in the Solar System
The Planet with Craters

Astronaut Rides Rover on Mars
The Planet with Rings
A Spacecraft

_____
_____
_____

_____
_____
_____

_____
_____
_____

_____
_____
_____

Name _____ Date _____

BUILDING SCIENCE VOCABULARY, WRITING SKILLS

Pretend that you are exploring another planet. During
your trip you write a letter to a friend about the planet.
Fill in this letter with your ideas.

Date _____

Dear _____,

I landed on _____. The first thing I

did _____. After

that I walked _____.

The best thing about this planet is _____

_____.

The worst thing about this planet is _____

_____.

While walking on the planet, I found _____.

It looks like _____. I think it

must _____.

I will spend 24 hours on the planet. I plan to _____

_____.

I hope to find out if _____

_____.

Sincerely,

_____

CHAPTER 12

ACTIVITY

PREPARING A CAPSULE FOR OUTER SPACE

Pretend you are working for NASA. You are preparing a capsule to send to outer space in a spacecraft. Your job is to find pictures and objects that would give an idea of what life is like on the earth.

A. You will need a large cardboard box, gold wrapping paper, a pencil, and several sheets of paper.

B. Cover the box with the gold paper. This will be your space capsule, and you will find items that can be placed in it.

C. On a separate sheet of paper, list objects you think would tell extraterrestrials something about life on the earth. Here are a few ideas:
1. Bird and animal sounds
2. Sounds and pictures of machines such as cars, factories, and typewriters
3. A map of where the earth is located in the solar system
4. Pictures of living things (include as many different kinds of animals and plants as possible)
5. Recordings of music (classical, rock, country & western, etc.)

D. Gather the objects you have written on your list. For some of them you can use photographs (or draw your own pictures). For other items, such as animals' sounds, you may have to make recordings.

E. On a separate sheet of paper, list each item and why you chose it. Then place the list and all the objects in the capsule.

F. Compare the objects in your space capsule with those of your classmates.

CHAPTER 13

MAGNETS

Section 13-1. WHAT ARE MAGNETS?
Look at each picture. Then read the question below it. In the empty box next to each picture, draw an answer to the question.

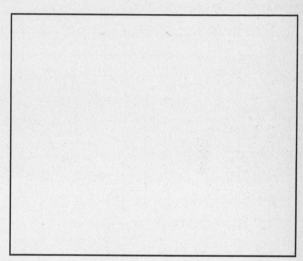

1. How could you get the paper clips out of the glass without touching the glass or spilling the water?

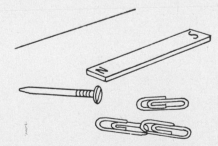

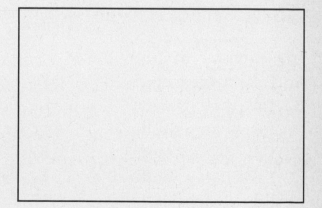

2. How could you make the iron nail act like a magnet so that it picks up the paper clips?

Section 13-2. HOW CAN WE USE MAGNETS?

Look at this treasure map. Each square stands for one step. Follow the step-by-step directions to find the buried treasure. Mark your steps with a crayon. The compass on the map will help you tell direction.

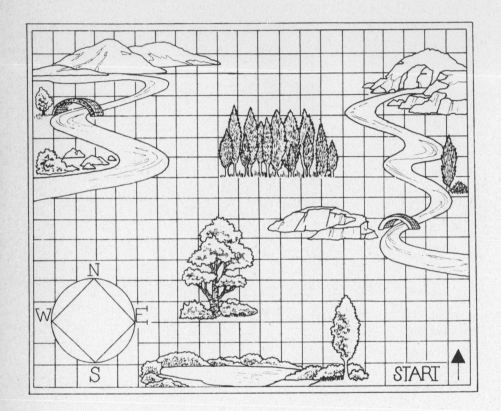

Directions:

A. Take 3 steps north.

B. Take 4 steps west.

C. Take 1 step north.

D. Take 5 steps west.

E. Take 1 step south.

F. Take 2 steps east.

G. Take 2 steps south.

H. Take 7 steps west.

I. Take 6 steps north.

J. Take 1 step east.

K. Take 6 steps north.

L. Take 8 steps east.

M. Take 2 steps north.

N. Take 3 steps east.

CHAPTER 13

SKILLS EXERCISE

CLASSIFYING

A. Here are three groups of objects. Circle the object in each group that can be picked up with a magnet.

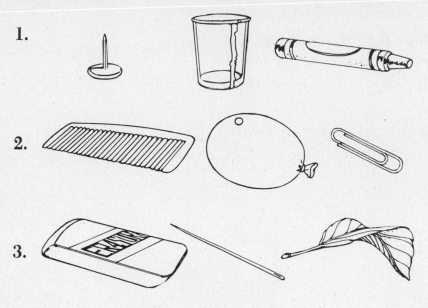

1.

2.

3.

FINDING THE MAIN IDEA

B. Here is a drawing of a compass. Add what is needed to make the compass complete.

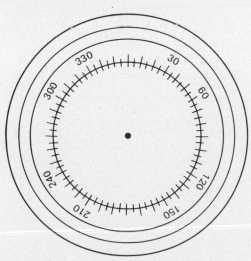

CHAPTER 13

ACTIVITY

CAN YOU USE A COMPASS?

A. Hide something in your classroom. Then get a compass, a sheet of paper, a pencil, and a meter stick.

B. Make a list of compass directions that a classmate can follow from the doorway of your classroom to the hidden object. Be sure to tcll how to go in each direction. For example, "Go 3 meters north. Then go 5 meters east."

C. Give the compass and the list of directions to a classmate.

CHAPTER 14

ELECTRICITY

Section 14-1. STATIC ELECTRICITY

A. These sentences about static electricity are missing some words. Fill in the blanks with the correct words from the list.

All _____ contains _____

charges. Charges can be _____ off objects.

When an object _____ or loses charges, it

has _____ electricity.

electric

gains

matter

rubbed

static

B. Every bit of matter contains millions of charges. There are two types of charges. There are positive charges (+), and there are negative charges (−). When matter has the same number of positive and negative charges, it has no static electricity. It is *neutral* (**new**-tril). If it has more positive charges, it is called *positive*. If it has more negative charges, it is called *negative*. Write *neutral*, *positive*, or *negative* next to each group of charges.

1. + + − + − +   _____

2. − − − + − −   _____

3. + + + + − −   _____

4. − − + + − +   _____

5. + + + − + +   _____

Name _____ Date _____

Section 14-2. ELECTRIC CURRENT

A. Look at these picture parts. Then answer the questions below.

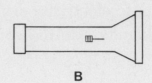

A   B

1. Which shows a closed circuit? _____

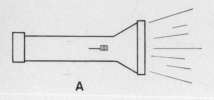

A   B

2. Which shows an open circuit? _____

B. In the space below, write a paragraph that describes the differences between an open circuit and a closed circuit.

_____

_____

_____

_____

_____

_____

_____

_____

_____

Name _____ Date _____

Section 14-3. SAFETY WITH ELECTRICITY

These pictures show some safety and conservation rules.
Write the rule that should be followed for each picture in
the space provided.

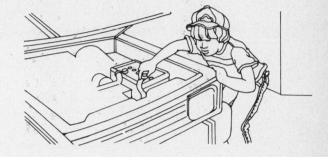

1. _____

_____

_____

2. _____

_____

_____

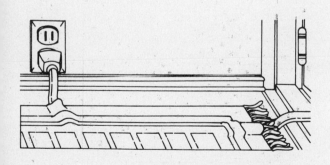

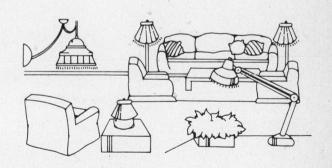

3. _____

_____

_____

4. _____

_____

_____

CHAPTER 14

SKILLS EXERCISE

PREDICTING

A. Imagine that you had a box that contained these circuit parts.

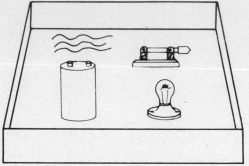

1. Would you have enough parts for a complete

   circuit? _____

2. If you answered yes, draw your circuit below.

B. Look at each of these boxes. Predict whether you could build a complete circuit with each. Explain your answers.

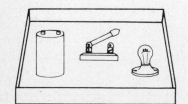   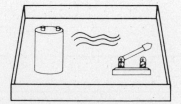

_____   _____

BUILDING SCIENCE VOCABULARY, WRITING SKILLS

Write a sentence using each of the words or phrases below.

1. charges _____
   _____
   _____

2. circuit _____
   _____
   _____

3. conductors _____
   _____

4. dry cell _____
   _____

5. open circuit _____
   _____
   _____

6. insulator _____
   _____
   _____

7. closed circuit _____
   _____
   _____

8. electric current _____
   _____

CHAPTER 14

ACTIVITY

MAKING A LIGHT BULB TELEGRAPH

You can make a light bulb telegraph. Letters of the alphabet are represented by dots and dashes in Morse code. Dashes are long buzzes sounded by the telegraph. Dots are short buzzes. With the light bulb telegraph, you will use long and short bursts of light instead of buzzes.

A. You will need bell wire 50 cm (20 in.) long, scissors, a flashlight bulb in a socket, a dry cell, a wooden or plastic movable clothespin, two unpainted thumbtacks, and tape.

B. Connect the parts of a circuit as shown in drawing **1.**

C. Attach the thumbtacks and wire to the clothespin as shown in drawing **2.**

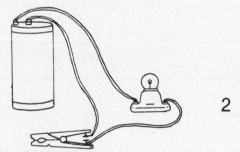

1

D. Press down on the end of the clothespin so that the thumbtacks touch. The light bulb should light.

E. You can send light messages using the Morse code. You can find the Morse code in a library book or encyclopedia.

2

CHAPTER 15

USING ELECTRICITY

Section 15-1. CHANGING ELECTRICITY
Section 15-2. MAKING AND CONSERVING ELECTRICITY

A. There are many things in your school that change
electricity. In the spaces below, draw two things that
change electricity. Then, explain what each does.

1. _____

_____

_____

_____

2. _____

_____

_____

_____

B. These pictures show two different ways to make
electricity. On a separate sheet of paper, write a short
paragraph about the kind of energy that makes the
electricity.

Section 15-3. COMPUTERS, BIONIC ARMS, AND OTHER AMAZING THINGS

A. Four parts of a computer are shown below. Write the correct name of the part under each picture.

1. _____

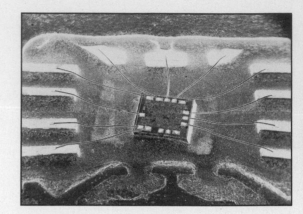

2. _____

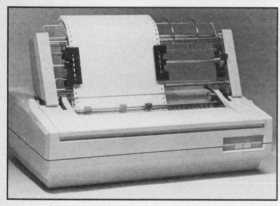

3. _____

4. _____

B. Using complete sentences, write what each part does.

1. _____

2. _____

3. _____

_____

4. _____

Name _____ Date _____

CHAPTER 15

SKILLS EXERCISE

BUILDING SCIENCE VOCABULARY
Read the definitions below and write the correct words in the puzzle.

ACROSS
1. A thin wire in a light bulb.
2. A material that does not burn but can be used to make electricity.
3. A magnet made by electricity.
4. A place where electricity is made by using uranium.
5. Something that can be burned.

DOWN
6. Using electricity to help the body work.
7. A tiny part of a computer; it has many circuits.
8. The part of a computer you type on.
9. A computer part that makes copies of what you typed.
10. The part of a computer that shows what you typed.

CHAPTER 15

ACTIVITY

MAKING A WET CELL

Batteries are usually made with dry chemicals. It is also possible to make a battery using the wet chemicals in a lemon.

A. You will need a lemon, a strip of copper, a strip of zinc, a plastic knife, bare wire 180 cm (72 in.) long, the earplug from a transistor radio, and a hole punch.

B. Roll the lemon on the table to soften it.

C. Cut two pieces of wire 90 cm (36 in.) long. Attach one wire to each metal strip as shown in drawing 1.

D. Make two slits in the lemon about 2.5 cm (1 in.) apart. In one slit place the strip of copper. In the other slit place the strip of zinc, as shown in drawing 2.

E. Place the earplug in your ear.

F. Wrap the end of one wire around the metal at the other end of the earplug.

G. With the end of the other wire, stroke the metal end of the earplug.

1. What do you hear? _____

The crackling sound means there is an electric current moving through the wires. Try to find out how your lemon is like a wet cell.

1   2   3

CHAPTER 16

THE FOREST AND THE GRASSLAND

Section 16-1. THE FOREST

Below are pictures of animals that live in the forest.
Under each picture, write the name of the animal. Then,
on a separate sheet of paper, write a short paragraph
about each animal. Tell what the animal eats and where it
lives.

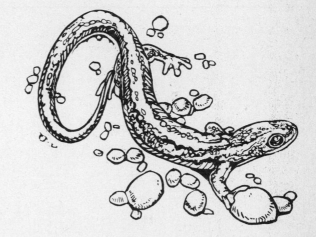

1. _____

2. _____

3. _____

4. _____

Section 16-2. THE GRASSLAND

In the box below, draw a picture of a grassland. Label the
plants and animals. You can color your drawing if you
wish. You should include these plants and animals:
grasses, wildflowers, grasshoppers, mice, meadowlarks,
cutworms, coyotes, and prairie dogs. You may also want to
include other plants and animals that you know about. Be
sure that all are kinds that live in a grassland. Before you
begin to draw, look at the pictures in your text and in
other books.

CHAPTER 16

SKILLS EXERCISE

BUILDING SCIENCE VOCABULARY, COMPARING AND CONTRASTING

A. Below are science words that were used in this chapter. Unscramble each word. Then write a sentence that tells what the word means.

1. DNE _____

_____

2. TABTAHI _____

_____

3. ORWUBR _____

4. LEHSRET _____

_____

B. Write a paragraph that describes how a forest and a grassland are alike and how they are different.

_____

_____

_____

_____

_____

_____

_____

CLASSIFYING

Below are pictures of animals that you learned about in
Chapter 16. Draw a square around each animal that lives
in a forest. Draw a circle around each animal that lives in
a grassland.

CHAPTER 16

ACTIVITY

OBSERVING MEALWORMS

Mealworms are another kind of animal that lives in grassland areas. Mealworms are not really worms. They are the young of a type of beetle. Mealworms eat cereal or grain. Sometimes they live in the flour and grain in bakeries and granaries. You can buy mealworms at most pet stores where fish are sold.

A. You will need mealworms, a shoe box, plastic wrap, green leaves, small pieces of paper, and some bran flakes.

B. Place a pile of green leaves in one corner of the shoe box. Put some bran flakes in another corner. Put small pieces of paper in a third corner.

C. Place 6 mealworms in the middle of the shoe box. Then cover the box with plastic wrap. Watch the mealworms move.

1. Where did the mealworms go? _____

_____

2. Do you think the mealworms used anything as a guide as they moved? _____

_____

3. Why did the mealworms go under the leaves, bran, and paper? _____

D. Leave the mealworms in the box overnight.

4. Where were the mealworms in the morning? Why?

_____

_____

5. What type of grassland animal might eat mealworms?

_____

CHAPTER 16

ACTIVITY

HOW DOES A TREE CHANGE?

The plants and animals in a habitat do not stay the same all year long. Do you know how they change? Here is a way to observe changes in nature.

A. Pick a tree that is in your school yard or near your home. Ask your teacher or another adult to help you find out what kind of tree it is. Then write the

name in this space. ————————————————

B. On a separate sheet of paper, draw a picture of the tree. Write the date of your first visit to the tree on your picture.

C. Carefully look at the tree. Then describe each part listed below. Include colors, shapes, and sizes.

1. Bark and trunk ————————————————

2. Leaves ————————————————

3. Branches ————————————————

4. Insects or birds living near or in the tree ————

————————————————

D. Visit the tree every 2 or 3 weeks for a period of several months. On a separate sheet of paper, carefully record any changes you see in the tree or in the animals that live in or near it.

E. Draw pictures that show changes you have seen in the tree. Be sure to write the date on each drawing.

F. After 3 months have passed, look at your drawings and notes. Then prepare a short report for your class about the changes you have observed.

CHAPTER 17

THE DESERT AND THE TUNDRA

Section 17-1. THE DESERT

The cactus is a source of water for some of the animals that live in the desert. Some of the parts of the cactus that help it live in the desert are listed at the left. The list at the right tells how these parts help the cactus. Draw a line from each part to the words that describe how it helps the cactus.

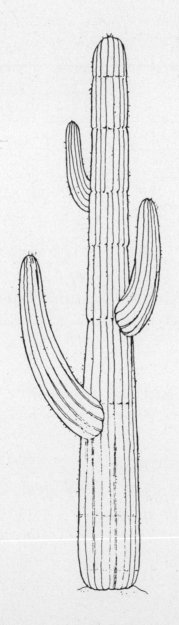

Thorns

Help cactus soak up rainwater quickly

Thick skin and no leaves

Protect the plant from animals

A stem or trunk that swells

Helps the plant store water

Roots underground but close to the surface

Keeps the plant from losing needed water

Name _____ Date _____

Section 17-2. THE TUNDRA

Use the clues listed below to complete the crossword
puzzle.

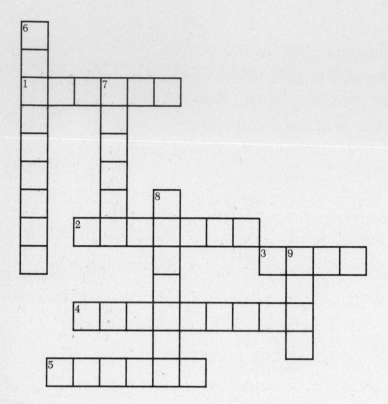

ACROSS
1. A very cold habitat.
2. A type of deer that roams across the tundra in the
   summer.
3. To become unfrozen.
4. An arctic bear.
5. A plant that can grow on rocks or rocky soil.

DOWN
6. An arctic bird that changes color.
7. A grassy plain that is frozen most of the year.
8. To move from one place to another.
9. A large group of animals.

CHAPTER 17

SKILLS EXERCISE

CLASSIFYING

Below is a list of plants and animals. Some live in the desert. Others live in the tundra. Read the list. Then write the names of the plants and animals in the correct column.

cactus	tortoise	sidewinder snake
moss	lichen	arctic poppy
arctic fox	caribou	ptarmigan
jackrabbit	mesquite	kangaroo rat
lemming	chuckwalla lizard	Gila woodpecker

DESERT   **TUNDRA**

_____   _____

_____   _____

_____   _____

_____   _____

_____   _____

_____   _____

_____   _____

_____   _____

_____   _____

CHAPTER 17

ACTIVITY

CAN YOU RAISE DESERT SHRIMP?

Rainfall on the desert may form water holes. The water in these holes may be salty because there is dry salt on the land. Salt water is called brine. Small animal eggs that were on the dry sand hatch in the salty water. These animals are brine shrimp. You can hatch brine shrimp.

A. You will need a large bowl, 2 large baby food jars, brine shrimp eggs that you can buy at a pet store, salt that is not iodized, a magnifying glass, a tablespoon, and dry yeast.

B. Make salt water by adding 15 ml (1 tablespoon) of salt to 500 ml (1 pt) of water. Let the water stand for 24 hr.

C. Fill each jar 3/4 full with salt water. Then add a small amount of brine shrimp eggs to each jar. Place one jar in a warm place and the other jar in a cool place.

D. Use the magnifying glass to look at the brine shrimp each day.

E. Draw a picture of the brine shrimp on a separate sheet of paper. Put the date on your picture.

1. In which jar did the brine shrimp hatch first?

_____

F. If some of the water in the jars evaporates, add fresh water that has been standing for 24 hours. Do not add salt.

G. After one week add 2 grains of dry yeast every other day. The yeast is food for the shrimp.

2. How big did your shrimp grow? _____

_____

CHAPTER 18

WATER HABITATS

Section 18-1. THE OCEAN

In this section, you have learned about plants and animals that live in the ocean. In the box below, draw a picture of this habitat. Before you begin your picture, look at the pictures in your text and in other books about the ocean. Be sure to include these plants and animals in your drawing: *kelp, plankton* (several kinds), *blue whale, herrings,* and *anglerfish.* If you know about other plants and animals that live in the ocean, put them in your picture. Label each plant and animal. When you have finished, you may want to color your picture.

Section 18-2. THE SHORE

Three animals that live at the shore are listed below. In
the box below each name, draw a picture of the animal.
On the lines to the right of each picture, write a sentence
telling where the animal lives.

1. Sandpiper

2. Barnacle

3. Mole crab

Section 18-3. THE POND

A. Fill in the blanks with the correct words from the list.

bullfrog	mayflies
algae	yellow perch
dragonfly	habitat
pond	turtle
bullhead	diving beetles
water lilies	blue heron

A _____ is a small body of water. It is another

example of a _____. _____

and _____, which are tiny plants, float in
the water of a pond. A four-winged insect that lives in a

pond is the _____. _____

and _____ are other insects that you might
see at a pond. Two fish that live in a pond are the

_____ and the _____.

The _____ and the _____
are two animals that sleep in the mud during the winter.

The _____ is a large bird that grabs fish
with its beak.

B. On a separate sheet of paper, draw a picture of these
pond plants: *arrowheads* and *iris*. Label and color your
drawing. Do these plants grow in the water or at the

edge of a pond? _____

_____

CHAPTER 18

SKILLS EXERCISE

CLASSIFYING, READING ILLUSTRATIONS

In this chapter, you learned about plants that grow in or near water. Some of the plants grow in salty ocean water. Others grow in the fresh water of ponds. Still others grow near the edge of the water. Write the name of each plant. Then write 2 or 3 sentences about each plant, describing it and telling where it grows.

1. _____
   _____
   _____
   _____
   _____
   _____

2. _____
   _____
   _____
   _____
   _____
   _____

3. _____
   _____
   _____

CHAPTER 18

ACTIVITY

WHAT KINDS OF PLANTS GROW NEAR WATER?

A. Find a plant that is growing in or near some water. The water can be a stream, river, ocean, lake, or pond.

B. Carefully look at the plant. Then answer the following questions.

1. What is the name of the plant? You may ask an adult to help you find the name in a book about

   plants. _____

2. How tall is the plant? _____

3. How wide is the plant? _____

4. Does the plant have leaves and a stem? Describe

   these parts. _____

   _____

5. Does the plant have roots? If so, are they long

   or short? _____

6. Is the plant growing in soil? If so, what type

   of soil is it? _____

7. Is the soil wet or dry? _____

8. What other kinds of plants are growing near this

   plant? _____

   _____

C. On a separate sheet of paper, draw a picture of the plant you have been observing. Label your picture and show it to your classmates. Compare your plant with their plants.

CHAPTER 18

ACTIVITY

HOW ARE BULLFROGS DIFFERENT FROM TURTLES?
In this chapter you learned that bullfrogs and turtles live
in mud during the winter. Find out more about bullfrogs
and turtles in other books. Then write a story about a
bullfrog and a turtle who live in the same small pond. Be
sure to include how these animals are different and how
they are alike.

_____

_____

_____

_____

_____

_____

_____

_____

_____

_____

_____

_____

_____